Pianoworks
Duets 1

compiled and arranged by
Janet and Alan Bullard

MUSIC DEPARTMENT

OXFORD
UNIVERSITY PRESS

Great Clarendon Street, Oxford OX2 6DP, England

Oxford University Press is a department of the University of Oxford.
It furthers the University's aim of excellence in research, scholarship,
and education by publishing worldwide

Oxford is a registered trade mark of Oxford University Press
in the UK and in certain other countries

First published 2012

1 3 5 7 9 10 8 6 4 2

ISBN 978–0–19–337835–3

Music and text origination by Julia Bovee
Printed in Great Britain on acid-free paper by
Halstan & Co. Ltd., Amersham, Bucks.

The *Pianoworks Duets 1* CD was produced by Andrew McKenna Music.

Preface

Welcome to *Pianoworks Duets 1*.

We hope you will enjoy this opportunity to play piano duets with a friend or teacher. Duet playing will help to develop your musical awareness and your ensemble playing, and it will be a lot of fun too!

To play piano duets comfortably, use either a piano duet stool or two stools/chairs placed as close together as possible (some players like to put their piano stool with the shorter edge facing the keyboard to save space). Middle C marks the dividing line between you, though you will often find your music goes above or below that note.

The music for the player sitting on the right-hand side (playing the upper notes) is called primo and the music for the player sitting to the left is called secondo. In this book the primo and secondo parts are printed on facing pages, although in some publications they are printed above and below each other. Always remember to look at the clefs carefully: the primo is often, but not always, in the treble clef for both hands (sometimes with an 8va/octave higher instruction for the right hand), and the secondo uses the bass clef more often than in solo music. In this book, as both parts of each duet are of roughly equal technical difficulty, you can experience using both clefs in each hand by taking it in turns to play the secondo and primo parts. The suggested fingerings should suit most players, but they are only suggestions—every hand is different.

The notes for the two players sometimes get very close together. To avoid getting in each other's way, make sure that you move your hands away when you are not playing. Using appropriate fingering will sometimes also help to avoid collisions.

It is usual for the secondo player to control the pedals because, generally, the secondo part contains the harmony, which dictates the use of the sustaining pedal. In this book, pedalling is not indicated on the score, although we have made a few suggestions for its use in the accompanying notes.

Keeping together—particularly starting together—can be a challenge for duet players. At first you might like to count yourselves in, but it's better to 'feel' the pulse together and to watch each other's hands so that the attack is carefully co-ordinated.

As you practise, be aware of which player has to project the melody and which player has the supporting accompaniment—the key to effective balance in duet playing is careful listening and adjusting.

With this book we have provided a digitized CD of the individual parts (sometimes with slower and faster versions) so that you can play each part with a 'virtual' pianist. Although not completely representative of a live performance, we hope the CD will be useful for practice, and that you will find the opportunity to duet with a 'real' pianist as well.

Good luck, and enjoy your duet playing!

JANET AND ALAN BULLARD

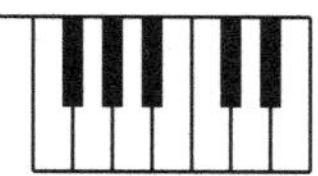

Contents

All pieces are original compositions or arrangements by Janet and Alan Bullard.

Agincourt Song

15th-cent. English

This song celebrates the British victory at the Battle of Agincourt in northern France and was possibly sung by Henry V's returning troops. In the primo part, lightly lift the staccato notes to communicate the music's dance-like quality.

Agincourt Song

15th-cent. English

Morning has broken

Trad. Scottish

This beautiful folk melody was collected from a Scottish singer in the nineteenth century and named 'Bunessan' after the village on the island of Mull. The words 'Morning has broken' were added in the early twentieth century. In the primo part, sustain the sound with legato phrasing, as if you were singing. The secondo part should be played very gently, particularly at the beginning, to support the melody.

Morning has broken

Trad. Scottish

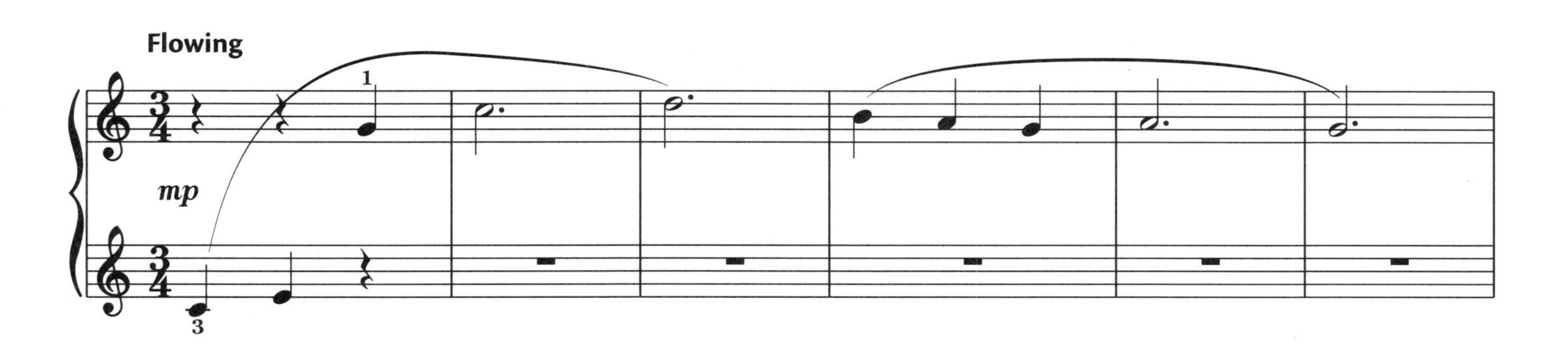

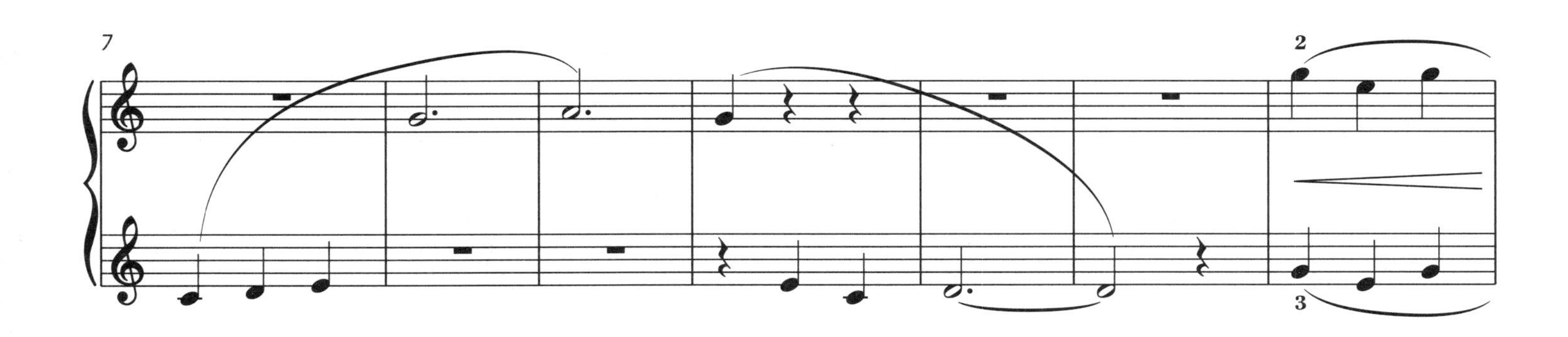

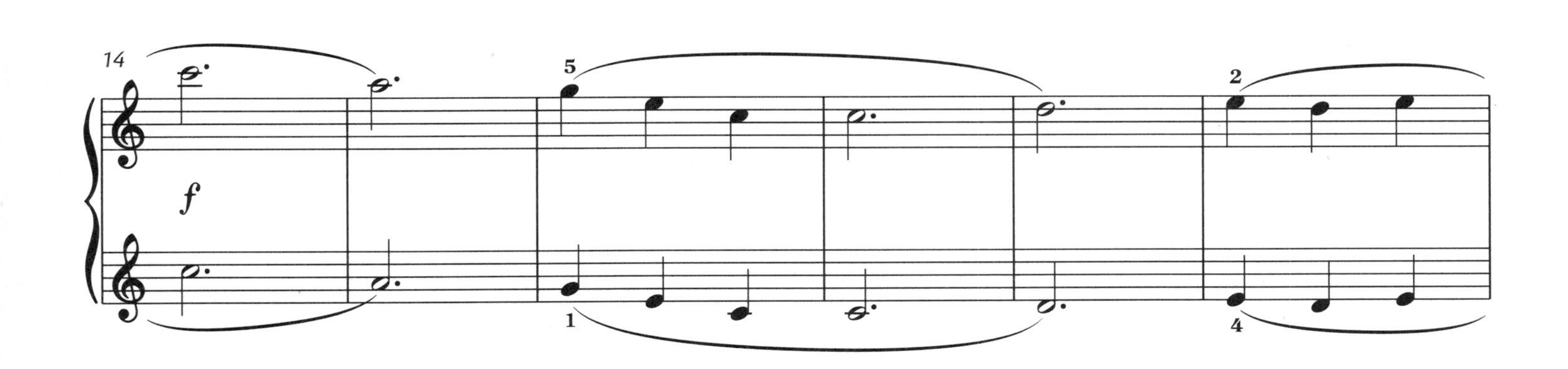

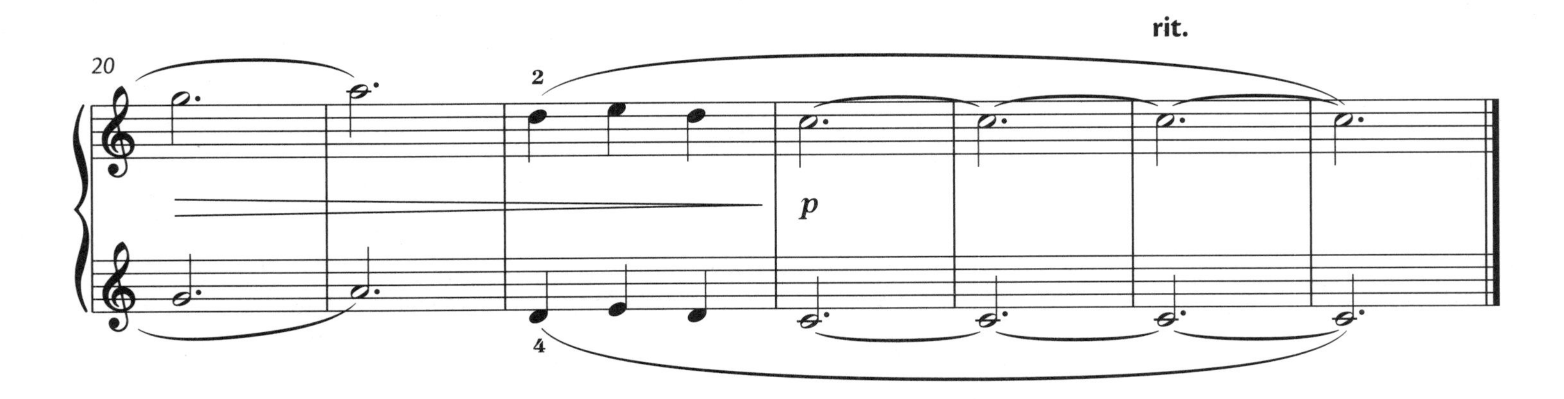

Norwegian Song

Trad. Norwegian
arr. Alan Bullard

Based on a fragment of a Norwegian shepherd's song, this piece stays in the same five-finger position throughout, with the addition of some sharps in the primo part. Aim for a sense of expressive flow in the outer sections, with a robust and joyful feel in the middle.

Norwegian Song

Trad. Norwegian
arr. Alan Bullard

The Entertainer

Scott Joplin
(c.1867–1917)

This is one of the most popular of Joplin's ragtime pieces, and its syncopated rhythms enlivened many gatherings in early twentieth-century America. In this version it is arranged as a conversation between the two players, so always project the tune when you have it, keeping the accompaniment quieter.

The Entertainer

Scott Joplin
(c.1867–1917)

Steady rag-time

mp

mf

p

mf

p

mf

p

mp

8va

f

f

mf

f

* Alternatively the As in this bar (and bars 9 and 13) can be played by the thumb of the left hand.

Amazing Grace

Trad. American

Set to an eighteenth-century text, this tune first appeared in an early nineteenth-century American shape-note collection, in which differently shaped note heads are assigned to each note of the scale. The deep sincerity shown in both the words and the music have ensured its undying popularity ever since. The primo player should keep the opening chords quiet, allowing the secondo melody to sing through, before taking over the tune in bar 16. From bar 17 the secondo player could add the sustaining pedal on the first two beats of each bar to enhance the texture.

Amazing Grace

Trad. American

SECONDO track 11 Secondo part only (slow tempo)
track 13 Secondo part only (fast tempo)

La Moresca

Tylman Susato
(c.1510–c.1570)

Susato was a wind player, composer, and publisher based in Antwerp, and this lively dance was one of his most popular works. The 'Moresca' was a fashionable dance during the Renaissance, and the English Morris Dance is one of its most enduring forms. In this arrangement, notice how the sustained middle section contrasts with the light and bouncy staccatos elsewhere.

La Moresca

Tylman Susato
(c.1510–c.1570)

SECONDO

track 15 Secondo part only (slow tempo)
track 17 Secondo part only (fast tempo)

Rondo

from Sonatina Op. 163 No. 1

Anton Diabelli
(1781–1858)

This spirited movement, slightly simplified in this arrangement, is one of many enjoyable duets that the Austrian composer and publisher Diabelli wrote for his piano students. Play the staccatos crisply to achieve a light sound, and really enjoy the wide dynamic contrasts. ***fp*** (forte piano) means play loudly and then immediately quietly—like an emphatic accent.

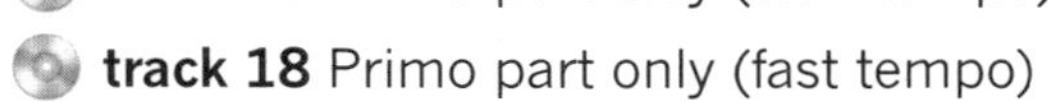

Rondo

from Sonatina Op. 163 No. 1

Anton Diabelli
(1781–1858)

SECONDO

Koinobori

Trad. Japanese

This Japanese folk song is traditionally sung on 5 May, 'Children's Day', when families hoist cloth streamers in the shape of carp ('koinobori') into the air to honour their children. This piece uses a five-note (or pentatonic) scale, so you could play it on the black notes only in the key of F sharp major, making every note into a sharp.

Koinobori

Trad. Japanese

Floating, drifting

Alan Bullard
(b. 1947)

Jazz waltzes are often played with swung quavers, but this piece works well with expressively shaped straight (even) quavers. While keeping the rhythm steady, aim to capture the free-flowing and relaxed character. Let the secondo melody sing through in bars 15–17, and aim for a general build towards the climax in bars 19–22, before dying away in the final bars.

Floating, drifting

Alan Bullard
(b. 1947)

Symphony No. 7

theme from the second movement

Ludwig van Beethoven
(1770–1827)

The slow second movement of Beethoven's Symphony No. 7 demonstrates the composer's masterly skill in creating dramatically convincing music from just a few repeated notes. Count silently at the beginning, watching each other to ensure that bar 3 is together, and then keep listening carefully for uniformity in the staccatos. In bar 19, allow the new idea in the secondo part to sing through with confident legato phrasing.

Symphony No. 7

theme from the second movement

Ludwig van Beethoven
(1770–1827)

SECONDO

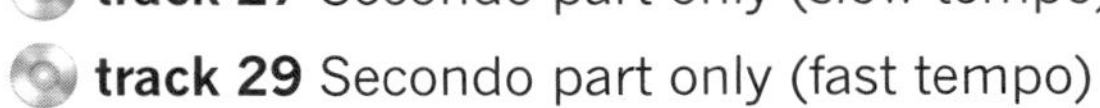

The Blue Danube

Johann Strauss II
(1825–99)

Probably the most popular of Strauss's waltzes, this piece will be most effective when played with particular attention to the contrasting articulation and gradual dynamic growth. When the triumphant climax is reached in bar 24, the primo player can enjoy taking over the melody with full tone.

The Blue Danube

Johann Strauss II
(1825–99)

track 31 Secondo part only

Pavane d'Angleterre

Claude Gervaise
(*fl.*1540–60)

The French composer Claude Gervaise wrote many instrumental dances, which were admired for their bright character and clear rhythm. Make the most of the dynamics to achieve an exciting echo effect, and really enjoy the accents at the end!

Pavane d'Angleterre

Claude Gervaise
(*fl.*1540–60)

Steady and smooth

f *p* 8 *f* 5 1 *p* 14 5 1 *f* *p* *f* 21 5 *p* 1 *f* 28 *p* 5 *f* 1 *ff*

SECONDO

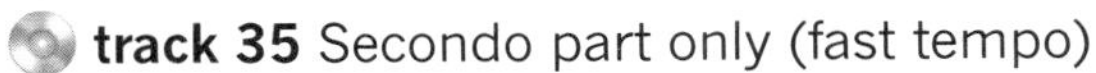

Symphony No. 104 ('London')

theme from the fourth movement

Joseph Haydn
(1732–1809)

Commissioned by the London-based impresario Johann Peter Salomon, this rousing work was Haydn's last symphony. On the surface, it features a simple rustic character and a drone bass—perhaps harking back to Haydn's youth, spent in a small Austrian village. Note that in bar 5 and bar 9 the melody is shared between the secondo and primo parts, so take care to balance the sound evenly. In bar 30 the primo player should clear the middle C in the left hand promptly so that the secondo player can take over the note in the next bar.

Symphony No. 104 ('London')

theme from the fourth movement

Joseph Haydn
(1732–1809)

SECONDO

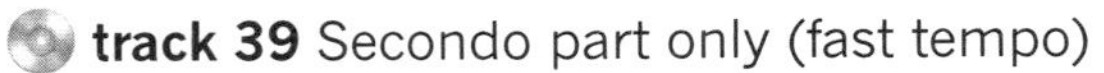

Hello Jamaica!

Alan Bullard
(b. 1947)

Enjoy the lively syncopations of this calypso-style piece, in which tight and accurate rhythms—with steady crotchets and minims in the secondo part—are more important than sheer speed!

 **track 38** Primo part only (slow tempo)
track 40 Primo part only (fast tempo)

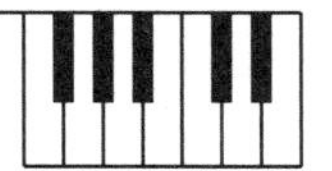

Hello Jamaica!

Alan Bullard
(b. 1947)

Happy and rhythmic

Valse lente

from *Coppélia*

Léo Delibes
(1836–91)

The story of the ballet *Coppélia* centres around a life-size mechanical doll that is so realistic that the townspeople believe she is a young girl, and one character, Franz, falls in love with her. This elegant waltz appears at the very beginning of the ballet when Coppélia is first sighted, and needs a gentle and responsive approach to communicate its character.

Valse lente

from *Coppélia*

Léo Delibes
(1836–91)

Go with the flow

Alan Bullard
(b. 1947)

In this tranquil piece, aim for a laid-back feel and a warm, even tone, with neat rhythms and a regular pulse throughout.

Go with the flow

Alan Bullard
(b. 1947)

SECONDO

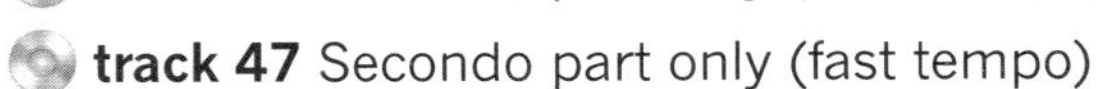

Can-Can

from *Orpheus in the Underworld*

Jacques Offenbach
(1819–80)

To enhance the energy of this lively dance, the opening section should be played delicately; the sudden fortissimos will then have their full effect later in the piece as the high-kicking dance steps take centre stage!

 **track 46** Primo part only (slow tempo)

track 48 Primo part only (fast tempo)

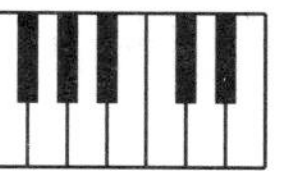

Can-Can

from *Orpheus in the Underworld*

Jacques Offenbach
(1819–80)

The John B. Sails

(Sloop John B.)

Trad. West Indian

Popularized by The Beach Boys under the title 'Sloop John B.', 'The John B. Sails' is a folk song from Nassau in the Bahamas. The syncopated rhythms in the primo part look a little complicated, but clapping them in preparation, while counting steady crotchets, will help the music to flow naturally and freely.

The John B. Sails

(Sloop John B.)

Trad. West Indian

On Wings of Song

Felix Mendelssohn
(1809–47)

Aim for expressively shaped legato phrasing in this gentle, lyrical song. To help with the sense of flow, finger changes have been suggested for some of the repeated notes in the primo part, but an alternative fingering may be used if preferred. The secondo player could also add some sustaining pedal wherever there is a dotted minim in the bass, with the pedal lifting towards the end of the bar.

On Wings of Song

Felix Mendelssohn
(1809–47)

Sweet and Low

Joseph Barnby
(1838–96)

As the director of music at Eton College, and later principal of the Guildhall School of Music, Barnby was a busy composer, conductor, and educator. The lullaby 'Sweet and Low' is one of his best-known choral songs and, although criticised by some for its over-sentimentality, it has nevertheless stood the test of time. Note that the quavers in the secondo part set the speed at the beginning. In the final bars, aim to synchronize the pause and the *rallentando* by 'thinking' the pulse and watching each other's fingers.

Sweet and Low

Joseph Barnby
(1838–96)

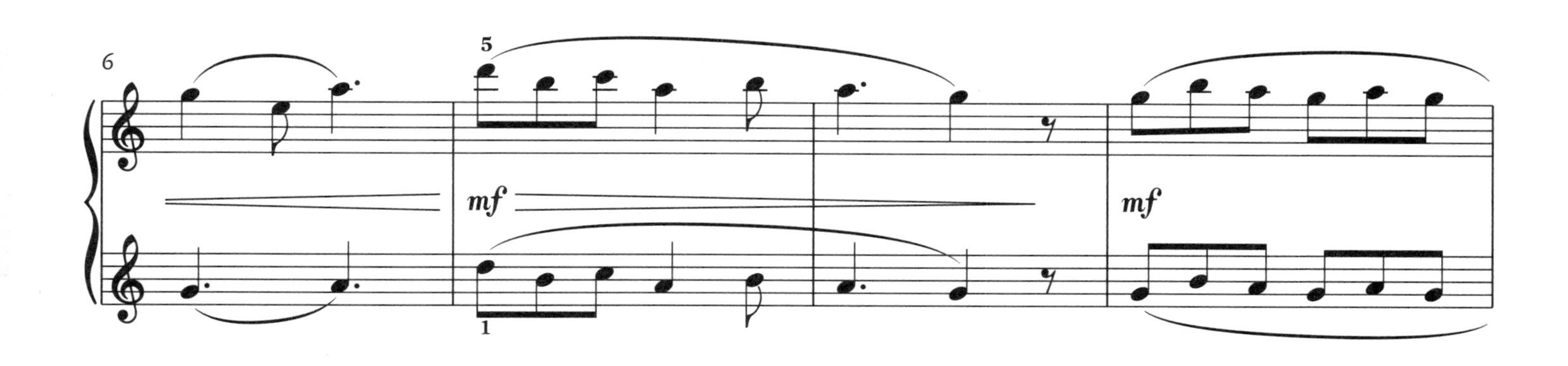

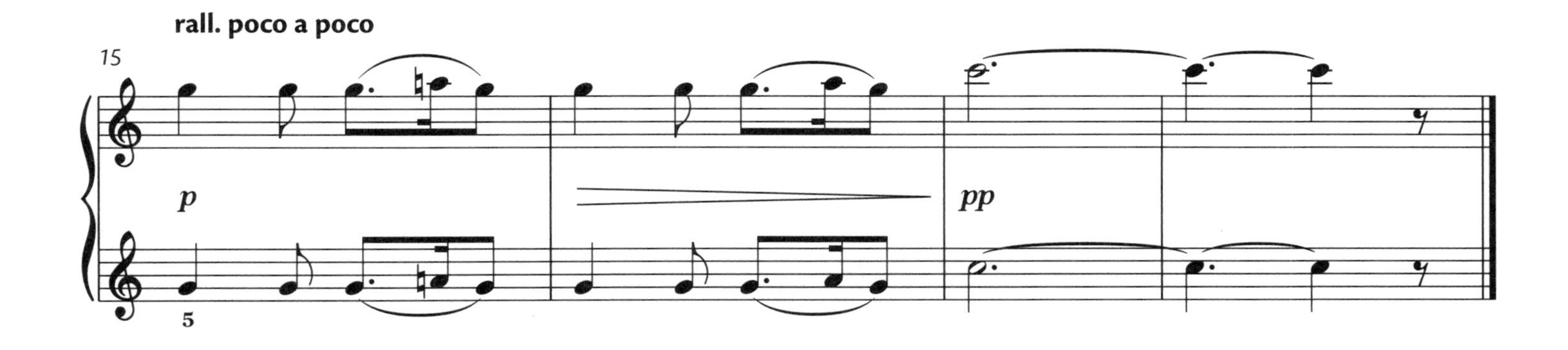

SECONDO

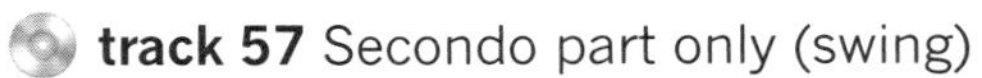

Five Finger Fever

Alan Bullard
(b. 1947)

Medium Tempo (straight or swing)

This piece can be played in two ways: with straight quavers or with swing quavers (where the first quaver of each pair is longer than the second). Whichever you use, the five-finger patterns need lots of energy as the dynamic level builds.

Five Finger Fever

Alan Bullard
(b. 1947)